To Alison

My dear long time
friend

Love Lorraine
2014

TO THOSE WHO KNEW ME WELL

By Lorri Starr

Copyright © 2007 by Lorri Starr

ISBN 0-7414-4302-3

Published by:

INFIN ITY
PUBLISHING.COM

1094 New DeHaven Street, Suite 100
West Conshohocken, PA 19428-2713
Info@buybooksontheweb.com
www.buybooksontheweb.com
Toll-free (877) BUY BOOK
Local Phone (610) 941-9999
Fax (610) 941-9959

Printed in the United States of America

Printed on Recycled Paper

Published December 2007

In the year 2000 alone there were 19 in 100,000 young people from 25 to 29 years old in Alberta who committed suicide. *Statistics Canada reports that more young Canadians die from suicide than by any other cause, except for accidents. Most of those are males. Most of these suffer from depression or other mental disorders.

*By Julia Nunes, Chatelaine (February 2005).

In this chronicle a mother expresses her and her son's feelings as they went through life together, before and during the illness.

My book is dedicated to my family and friends who described the changed circumstances that this young man experiences in their presence. I am hoping that Chad's life will help family and friends understand how depression affects so many young people. We all need to be aware of the signs that exist during depression.

EARLY DAYS

Mom: Dr. Boyd was the assisting obstetrician. He was a younger man with dark hair and glasses. Because the baby inside me was developing and growing at an advanced level, the doctor decided to hook me up to an IV drip to help induce labour. I was pacing the hallways of the older General hospital, which was only two blocks from our first family home. Labour took two days. Can any human being imagine pushing for that length of time?

Ten pounds, one ounce! Wow! January 10, 1973, Chad Stephen was born in the General Hospital in Cardelle. Sharon, a young lady I had attended school with, happened to be the nurse on duty that day. She came into my room to announce "we made a mistake. Your gorgeous son is ten pounds, not ten pounds and one-ounce." Talk about having the big one!

That one-ounce didn't make any difference. He was healthy and beautiful. I was elated.

Baby's older brother, Paul, was already four years old. Chad's birth was just as exciting as Paul's was. Chad was so handsome. He had chipmunk cheeks and big brown eyes. Ralph, his dad, brought in a sleeper for the baby to wear home. I must admit that I felt cheated because our baby already fit into a size four-month sleeper.

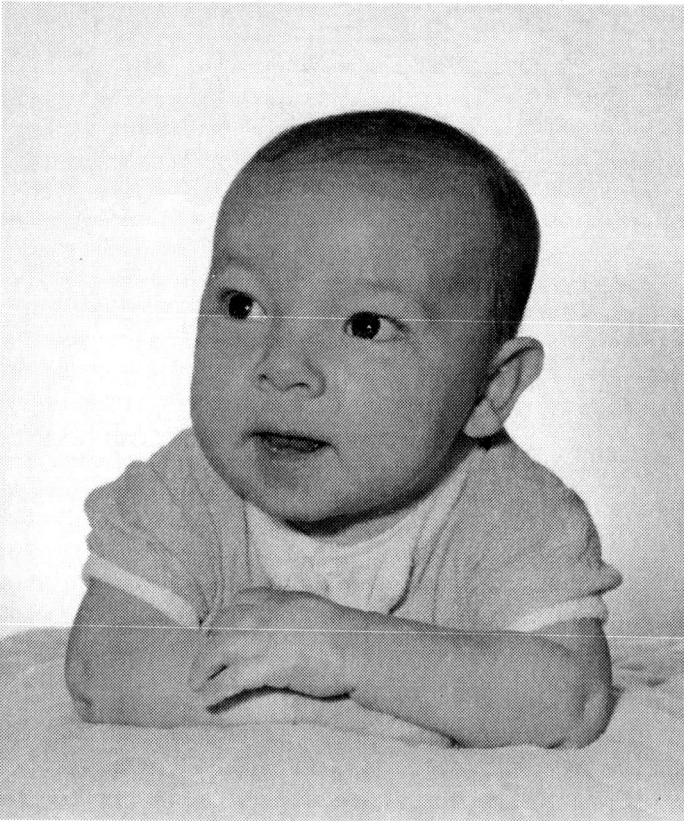

Chad Stephen-Four Months Old

◆◆◆◆◆◆

I recall that winter of 1973 very well. The snow had reached astounding heights while I was in the hospital. Ralph, my husband, had to shovel the snow behind the garage to get the car out. The roads hadn't been ploughed yet so it was hard to drive home. Chad was beginning his life journey.

Our family's first home was a very small, pink, stucco house downtown. It was very old, but the rent was cheap and it had a fenced yard for the boys to play in.

The house was so decrepit, that it was a hazard. The ceiling in the living room fell in twice. Who said the sky doesn't fall?   The house was two stories high, with the washing machine in the basement.   I kept getting electrical shocks from the power plug connected to the washing machine.

I was going downstairs to fetch a load of laundry from the dryer. I don't know why I thought that if I partially closed the basement door that Chad would be safe.   He nudged the door wide open and catapulted all the way down the stairs, still in his walker.   It's so heartbreaking to see your child shriek in pain and fear.

Chad was in the white plastic high chair looking at his second birthday cake on the table in front of him.   He was laughing non-stop at all this fun. Not understanding that the candles were to be blown out, he tried to snuff the flames with his little hands.

◆◆◆◆◆◆

A few years later my girlfriend, Joann and I were driving around in her metallic blue 1970 Ford Galaxy. The car in front of us jerked to a stop. Joann had to slam on the brakes. Chad was in the baby seat. Chad flopped out of the baby seat and was hanging upside down by the seat belt. All of us were shaken up and livid with the careless driver in front of us. After coming to grips with what just happened and checking Chad and Joann's two children, we all seemed to be OK.

Chad began to rock his head back and forth for hours at night. I have no idea when the head rocking stopped, if ever. It worried immensely about it and the paediatrician didn't have any explanation for the head rocking. I had visions of a grown man (Chad) head rocking while trying to have a relationship with a lady.

◆◆◆◆◆◆

When Chad had grown into an energetic, talkative two-year-old, we had another addition to our family. I also delivered this baby being induced with an IV drip. It was another long delivery. Actually, when he was ready to enter our world, a person could say he made a flash appearance. I told the nurses the baby was ready to arrive. The nurses weren't quite ready for this surprise. The baby was born on the stretcher as the stretcher was wheeled down the hallway to the delivery room.

Sorry, doc. The baby's already here. Your services are not needed now. Paul and Chad gained a baby brother. Both boys were delighted. They loved to play with their new brother, who we named Trent.

Chad, Trent and Paul

Shortly after, our family decided to buy a house in the Courtland district of the city. This was a much nicer neighbourhood, a residential area with lots of trees and flowers in the yards. This time our house was gray stucco with a large basement (including a basement suite that we rented out to people), and a garage in the back. There was a sizeable, slanting, fenced yard.

The boys would play on the swings, kick the big rubber ball, or splash in their turquoise patterned plastic pool. Ralph and I watched the boys play as we were repairing and painting the fence a bright white. It was so funny watching Chad trying to turn a somersault and landing on his side instead, then roll out of control down the sloped yard.

The boys had neighbourhood friends and other children accompanying them in their play most days. Would you believe the boys tried to drown a batch of poor baby kittens in a wash tub? That was typical boy behaviour, I guess. We caught the boys and their friends in time to rescue the kittens from a doomed life.

Chad: My grandparents (the Stephens), and the family that surrounded me were something greater than anything else I ever cared to know was. The wheat fields of my grandfather's farm seemed to reach out far beyond any world that I knew. And, for me at the time, it was more than I could ever want or need.

Draping both my waking hours and my dreams with more warmth and security that any child could help to carry. There were my parents, along with my two brothers, aunts, uncles and cousins.

In those days I had no cause for concern or belief that my future would take me as far as I feel only now from a universe I knew only as my own. There I was, as wide-eyed and curious as a young child can be. I was a happy little boy, filled with wonder and life, yet I couldn't have been more oblivious to the awe and magnitude of my surroundings. Like any five-year-old, everything to me was new with challenges. I'd either take the challenges on blindly, or had only the innate sense that they were too very ominous for my yet small presence.

◆◆◆◆◆◆

We had our traditional Christmas at home. My brothers and I helped make tree ornaments out of baking clay dough. That was always fun. Mom said she would keep the ornaments and put them on the tree every year.

We also spent part of our Christmas at our grandparents' home, in a small town in Sardonia... 400 miles away. Our cousins (who were boys our age) from the small city of Mentrade would also be at Sardonia, along with Uncle

George's family. It seemed that the whole town of Sardonia made an appearance at Grandparents Stephens' home during the holidays.

Fourth Christmas

My grandparents were Russian-Ukrainians. Their house was always laid out with delicious Ukrainian food. We were fed six times a day, usually gaining weight by the time we left for home.

We boys would grin ear to ear as we ripped the wrapping paper off our Christmas presents.

There was the always-comforting voice of my grand-father saying "Pocahontas (a childhood name he coined for me and carried well into my adulthood, until his passing).

"Pocahontas, what are you doing?" Grandpa Stephen always asked. He was one of my favourite people. I remember him hoisting me up and kissing me on the forehead.

He would take my brothers and me to Daily's cafe for a treat. My brothers called me Grandpa's "Golden Boy". I phoned and wrote to Grandpa often. He knew how much I loved him.

Grandpa would buy all kinds of clothes for us, usually from the good old "Army & Navy Surplus "store. Even if the clothes were too big, Grandpa's heart was still there. He didn't realize all the sewing Mom had to do, to make the clothes fit us. We boys fondly remember loading up the car with all our gifts of love from them, plus Grandma's sandwiches, cookies, fruit and drinks for the ride home.

◆◆◆◆◆◆

Mom: Things became very unsettled at home. Ralph was out drinking a lot. This caused a lot of pressure for the family.

Chad: Dad came home drunk so many times. Mom would scream at him because he kept belittling her and calling her names. Dad was trying to blame her for his drinking behaviour. One time he pitched his plate of food against the wall. We boys hid in the bedroom. Paul remembers blanking it all out of his mind because it was so painful. Continual fighting between Ralph and I finally ended in a divorce.

Mom: I moved the boys with me into another home (two blocks from Ralph's house). It was the main floor of a small house. It was an older house, but did have a large fenced yard for the boys to play in. The convenient part was that their school was across the street, and the daycare was next door to us. The basement had another suite in it where a young couple lived. They were quiet and never caused us any grief.

In spite of the boys being able to visit their dad at any time, Chad seemed to feel the family break-up the most. He was four at the time.

"Where's my Daddy?" Chad sobbed. It broke my heart to see the pain he suffered.

One day I packed up the boys into my tan 1970 Dodge Dart car and drove across the city to visit a lady friend. When we arrived back home it was very dark. The front door had been broken apart. It was on the frame, hanging haphazardly. Being scared out of my wits, we moved stealthily inside to check things out. Someone had stolen the mattresses off the boys' bunk beds! Who in the world would want just children's mattresses and nothing else? I purchased a new set of bunk beds and a single bed for the boys' bedroom. We never did find out who the thief was.

We stayed in that house until I finished my nurses training. I asked a few male friends to help move me to Lexton, but they never showed up in time. When I arrived home from school it was still daytime. The landlord had deposited all my furniture on the front lawn. Was I ever upset! The guys eventually did show up with their truck to help me move.

LEXTON

Mom: I didn't feel comfortable living so close to the ex-husband, so I moved to Lexton. In my later teenage years I had lived in Lexton and worked at the airport as a waitress and janitor.

Lexton had a lot of good memories for me, even though most of my former friends lived elsewhere now. We temporarily moved into a basement apartment in Lexton until I could finalize purchasing our home. We were evicted from that apartment building because the boys kept running up and down the halls and disturbing the other tenants. This all happened when I was trying to study for final exams in nursing school. What a nightmare!

Thank goodness the purchase of my new house became finalized at the same time. Studying and moving with three young boys was no picnic though. I was so, so distraught. On top of all this turmoil I had to settle the boys in a new school.

There was no landscaping or anything yet at our new home. We proceeded to have a mouth-watering T-bone steak barbeque on our wooden picnic table in the all dirt backyard. The seagulls even thought the leftovers were great. One bird swallowed a whole T-bone (with the meat chewed off already). We couldn't believe what we saw.

Where were the bird's table manners?

After fortunately passing my exams and receiving my licensed practical nurse's degree, the next thing to do was get accustomed to my new job. I went to work at the hospital right across the street. It was hard to find a babysitter. One evening shift when I had to work, one of my friends suggested a young fellow they knew for a babysitter. I left work early to go home because it was a slow shift. As I opened my apartment door, teens and beer bottles flew out of my apartment. There was a party going on. The cigarette smoke was unbearable. I wrote the babysitter a cheque, but stopped payment at the bank the next day. Why should I pay some teen that wasn't even aware that his job was to keep my boys safe and secure?

Chad's Seventh Birthday

Chad as a Cub Scout, 1980

Chad: Mom used to promise us boys' ice cream at McDonald's after church on Sunday (if we behaved). We were boys. We didn't think about what being good meant. We squirmed and giggled all through mass anyway. Mom wanted ice cream after mass as much as we did.

We only had to walk about three blocks to school. Seeing that Mom was Catholic, we were enrolled in Notre Dame Catholic School. We boys completed all the traditional Catholic sacraments. Father Dodd baptized us at St. Michael's Church. Mom now had a boyfriend, Larry, who became our new godfather. We were very active in church functions. Some of my best friends were from the church. The same priest confirmed me a few years later.

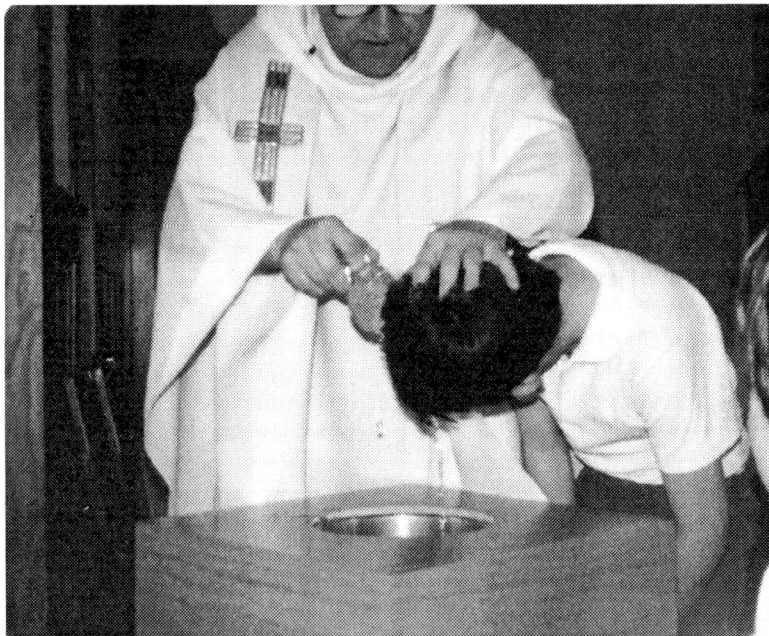

Baptism 1981

The next four years were fairly normal. Paul was four years older than I was so he had a bit of an advantage over us younger boys. He would make Trent and I dress up in winter clothes or hockey gear and fist pound the heck out of us. Paul used to chase us around the basement shooting at us with a BB gun.

◆◆◆◆◆◆

Mom and Larry were going on vacation for three weeks to Nova Scotia. We were dropped off at Grandma and Grandpa Marion's. They lived in a tiny trailer out in the country. That was special because we were so used to the big city life. There was even a river in town to go fishing.

Grandpa watched TV all the time. Grandma was great. She taught us to do leather work. I tooled Mom's name on a leather key chain. Mom loved it.

Grandma Marion taught us how to collect bottles to sell. We sold the bottles in the same store where we could buy candy. I was so indecisive. I wanted the most for my little money.

Mom: Then came the day Chad's paediatrician informed us that our son had an atrial-septal heart defect. That explained why Chad was always the first to tucker out when playing with his friends. He was also on the slim side. Dr. Deck explained that Chad would have to wait eight years before his heart could be operated on. I felt deep apprehension regarding Chad's condition. What would the next eight years bring? We made frequent trips to visit Dr. Deck to make sure that an operation would not have to be done any sooner. I remember how odd it seemed when Chad had to be hospitalized to have eighth teeth fixed.

The day of Chad's heart operation arrived. It was scheduled a few years ahead of time because the paediatric cardiac specialist was the only one Cardelle had and the doctor was moving to the USA soon. Being a licensed practical nurse myself, I was familiar with the usual pre-op routine.

One of my hobbies was painting yellow roses on a lace tablecloth. It was very intricate work and required concentration. I brought the tablecloth with me to the hospital to keep my mind occupied. I would paint, get up and pace, paint and so on. The day dragged on. Fear gripped the pit of my stomach.

During the eight-hour operation, Ralph and I weren't told much about how the operation was going. It was evening by the time the operation was over. We were allowed to go into go into intensive care to see Chad. My face blanched white as I saw my son lying there, hooked up to so many tubes. All we could do was wait vigil at his side until he woke up in the recovery room. We sighed with relief when he opened his eyes. The poor little guy didn't have a clue what was going on. The doctor told us there was nothing else we could do at this time. It was time to go home and rest.

Larry wasn't involved with Chad's heart operation, but his dad Ralph was. The next day Ralph and I entered Chad's room feeling fearful. Chad was sitting up in his bed and didn't seem in any distress. I had brought a bottle of Vitamin E for the nurses to administer to Chad. I wanted his foot-long chest suture to heal quickly and not be too noticeable. Chad would always be self-conscious of his scar.

Chad was home in a week. It's funny, but I felt an inner pride because he recuperated so well. That month he gained 20 pounds. He would now be able to live a normal life and keep up with playing with his friends. It was such a thrill to see him run and jump instead of lay on the couch, pale and worn out.

After a few years Larry became physically abusive to Mom. The day after he held a knife to her throat she packed his possessions and left them on the front door step.

◆◆◆◆◆◆

My best lady friend, Jill, lived on a farm about one hour from Lexton. It was fun to take the boys out there. They loved to ride all the All Terrain Vehicles and have some fun shooting at magpies. I slept in the second bedroom of the trailer and the boys bunked in the camper.

At Jill's Farm

Jill was outside early in the morning and heard the boys talking in their camper. Jill didn't know which boy said it, but she heard "did you eat all that damn corn? I wanted some."

We laughed about that for years.

Jill had two dogs, Beanie and Bony (golden retrievers). The dogs would perch on the white plastic picnic chairs on the trailer deck.

At night we had a roaring bonfire and some of the neighbours would join us. Jill was such a card. We couldn't help but have a blast when we visited her.

When we left we always I stocked the car up with country food. I usually bought a side of pork or beef from the town butcher. Jill heaped vegetables from the garden in boxes for me. I bought eggs and frozen chickens from her. We were well supplied for the next season.

◆◆◆◆◆◆

Chad: I was a bit of a firebug. Campfires would fascinate me. I sneaked closer to the flames to see where they came from. The red-hot coals burnt my feet. Trent and I played with matches and left the burnt ones all over Jean's (Ralph's common-law wife-our stepmother's) cabin. I remember hiding firecrackers in the plant pots in Jean's house in Cardelle.

At home in Lexton, Trent and I even put gas in tin cans and lit them on fire. Trent caught his pants on fire. The neighbours called an ambulance. By the time they got to our house Trent had the fire out and had hidden his pants in the garbage. Mom was still at work. When she got home the neighbours reported the fire to her but she never did find my burnt pants.

◆◆◆◆◆◆

I remember an assigned weekend we spent with Dad in Cardelle. When Mom came from Lexton to pick us up, he decided that we boys weren't going home with Mom. All Mom had done is request that we boys would continue to attend church services and be raised as Christians. Ralph went ballistic, feeling that I had no right to ask for any restrictions on raising our boys.

At that point Mom got frantic and told Dad to hit her if it would make him feel any better. It was a weird call but she felt he would calm down afterwards. Dad slapped her face real hard and gave her a black eye. We boys were petrified and didn't know what to do...hide or just keep watching. Mom went to work with her black eye the next day.

Mom: The next day Ralph had time to think about what he did and realized it would be too hard on the boys to be without me. Besides that, being with me was better that being with a babysitter everyday, while he worked.

◆◆◆◆◆◆

It seemed like Chad had such a hard time doing his homework. As soon as he arrived home from school, he sat at the kitchen table glued to his books. Chad would complete his homework before he even thought of playing with the other kids. It was a little peculiar to see a child so dedicated to schoolwork the way he was.

His brothers were much different. They would play until they thought they could get out of doing homework at all. The teachers set up a scribbler of assignments for Trent, to be sent home to me in order that I could check what homework he should complete each day and then sign it.

◆◆◆◆◆◆

I married September 11, 1983 to Barry Hilderman. He was a good-looking but slim fellow. He reminded me of Chuck O'Connor, the movie star. I wore a short white chiffon dress with lace on the bodice and a flared skirt. My wide brim hat sat delicately on top of my long, curly, black hair.

It was to be a little family wedding in Queen Elizabeth Park. Well, it rained that day. The Justice of the Peace had the basement of his home decorated for emergency situations like this. Thus, Barry and I married in a basement suite in Cardelle. My three boys and his two daughters and son were the only ones we asked to be with us that day. After the ceremony we went to the Boston Pizza for a small reception. Barry's girls gave Barry and me a hand-made congratulation card. That really touched my heart.

That night Barry and I had a gig playing disk jockey music at someone else's wedding. We took the opportunity to set up our reel to reel DJ music so that we could share the first dance with the other couple. The wedding couple chose the first three songs to dance to. After that, we chose three songs for the next three dances. I remember dancing to "Lady in Red." That song will always be a favorite for me. That was a unique memory in itself.

Barry taught me how to be a disk jockey and we each played music in a different place on the weekends. We played at all sorts of functions...weddings, teen dances, bars, Christmas parties and even a house warming.

Chad: I hated my stepfather. Barry thought because he was with Mom that he could tell us what to do. Well, he was not we boys' father and not my mother, so I didn't have to do a thing he said. He thought sticking us in our rooms when we didn't listen to him was something he had authority to do.

Mom: Life was OK for about six months. Barry's children only stayed with us on some weekends. I became very fond of them.

Chad: The youngest girl, Bonnie, would love to pinch and tease us boys. I got her back, pinching her one time, even though Mom taught us not to hit girls. Bonnie cried her head off. That was the beginning of the end for Mom's marriage. Thank God Mom got rid of Barry. It lasted for less than a year.

Mom: I found funding to send my sons to Circle Square Ranch. It was a rodeo camp. The boys learned some rodeo horse tricks.

Circle Square Ranch

◆◆◆◆◆◆

It was a religious camp, though. Paul, Chad and Trent learned a lot about right and wrong while they were there. Other children even began speaking in tongues (talking in an old religious dialect from years ago), as if a spirit possessed them. The boys were angels after camp was over. They came home determined to not even fight with each other. It was lovely, but unfortunately the good behaviour only lasted for about two weeks.

I borrowed a six-person tent from a lady friend of mine. Well, who ever decided six people could sleep in that size of a tent wasn't taking into consideration rainstorms. Paul was with his dad that weekend. My two sons who were with me at the time, were sleeping soundly, looking completely dead to the world. My friend and I finally had to creep into my dry, blue Ford LTD and sleep on the seats.

20

Jasper

The next day Chad and Trent were in awe. This was their first trip to the mountains. Just being on a holiday was a thrill for them.

◆◆◆◆◆◆

Chad: Mom was taking private guitar lessons from a young man. She went to the studio for lessons for a long time, around two years. Somehow I just had to get my hands on her guitar. She didn't want us (my brothers and me) touching it because she thought we would wreck the guitar. I kept bugging her and bugging her to let me try playing her guitar. She finally gave in.

Mom sent me to lessons when she realized my determination to play. I began lessons at a studio in Lexton. When we moved to Cardelle, one of Mom's friends (who had performed with the band "Powder Blues") gave me lessons in other types of music such as jazz and slow rock. That was all right. I loved playing hard rock the best, though.

Guess what? I mastered the guitar in six months. I must have gotten my musical talent from my Grandpa Stephen. Soon I began teaching guitar lessons to other people. What a blast! I got to have fun and make money, too.

Cadet Duty 1985

◆◆◆◆◆◆

Mom: I was standing in my kitchen looking out the window. I flipped around and noticed Chad rousting around in the cupboards looking for a snack. Suddenly a morbid thought crossed my mind. He's suicidal. I have no idea why I thought that. The notion vanished just as quickly as it came.

Chad: When I was 14 Paul had already moved in with Dad. Trent was spending about six months (or until he shaped up) in a group home for behaviour problems. Trent chose to live with Dad after his group home stretch.

Being the only son left with Mom, I thought I was going to have freedom and fun. Our house was so empty. I felt so alone...like I was the only person in the whole world. My Mom was working at Mount Pleasant Hospital, doing evening shifts

◆◆◆◆◆◆

We did some neat stuff...my friends and I. One night Carl Landart (my friend next door) and I discovered that the people across the street weren't home. All we had to do was walk into their house to lift a cassette recorder and a bunch of cassette tapes. The next day the police were asking questions. Carl and I refused to squeal on each other. The cops didn't discover who the thieves were. Mom was questioned about it but didn't know anything and hadn't seen any evidence at home. We boys had a private stash of things in Carl's garage.

I went to Dad's for the weekend. Mom wasn't home in Lexton either. Carl and his girlfriend stayed in our house all weekend. They were smart and didn't eat any of our food. Mom knew someone had been in the house but couldn't imagine whom.

Mom stashed money in a safe to pay bills and buy groceries. When she was at work, I busted into the safe and stole eighty-five dollars. Mom couldn't figure out why the money was gone and my brothers wondered how I acquired BB guns and all kinds of things. I told Paul and Trent that I had my sources.

My friend Warren Compton and I were twelve years old and partying with a bunch of friends. Man, we got smashed. We tried to ride our bikes home, but couldn't do it. We tried to push our bikes home. That didn't work either. Finally we crawled home on our knees. We were ready to beg for forgiveness before we even got home. Our pants were filthy and ripped.

Warren and I decided to play hooky. Goofing around was cool. We spent the day playing games at the arcade, hanging out, while the rest of our buddies were in school. Warren's dad, Gerry, found out and stormed down to the arcade to seize Warren away from there and back home. He asked Warren to get a switch. Warren could only find a huge stick.

Gerry said angrily that "I want to spank you, not kill you!"

Warren and I were bored and thought we should go for a drive. We snuck the van keys from his mom's coat in the front door closet. Warren and I pushed the van to the corner so Warren's parents wouldn't hear us. Man, did we have fun! We spun doughnuts all over the place. Oh, oh! We hit the curb. Something's broken. I think it's the axle. Now we're in trouble! Fear washed over us.

The only thing we could think of doing was talking to Lindsey, Warren's older sister. We hammered on Lindsey's front door. Lindsey was rubbing her eyes and drowsily said "What's wrong?"

Warren, gasping "Dad's going to kill us!

I took off home. I just hoped Mom wouldn't find out.

The van was left in the street overnight. In the morning, when Gerry and Rita (Warren's mom) went to get the van, there was terrible news. Gerry's tools worth $4000 had been stolen from the van. Gerry was ready to strangle us, but Sister Joan was visiting their home at the time. She kept things under control and saved Warren and I from too much punishment.

Billy, another friend, sometimes hung out with Warren and me. We used to sit around drinking and joking about how we were going to do ourselves in. Billy said he would use a nice strong pipe to hang himself.

A year later Billy did hang himself on a pipe in the bathroom. Adam, John and I made a pact that we would never, never commit suicide and put everybody through that pain! It was just too heartless.

◆◆◆◆◆◆

Mom: The house was too big to care for now. With my full time nursing job, selling Amway, and raising Chad, it just seemed too much. I mulled over selling the house and moving.

My present boyfriend, Ron, asked me to move in with him. It seemed that it was a good option. I waited six months to get to know him better.

I remember my tears of frustration, trying to get the house in tip-top shape to put it on the market. My ankle had been reset because of not healing properly from a previous injury. My foot was in a cast. I was attempting to do the sale on my own. I wanted the transition but without help, it was going to be too difficult. Finally, giving up, I hired Alnerth Reality to sell the house.

I felt so bad, asking Chad to decide whether he wanted to move in with Ron and me or live with his dad. He was 15 then. He chose to live with his dad and brothers. Ron's friend, Bob, helped Ron and I with the move.

NEW BEGINNING

Chad: I was ecstatic when I got to move in with Dad and transfer to Westrose Junior High School for grade nine.

A family with three children purchased Mom's house. The family went away for a weekend. The owners came back after the weekend and accused my brothers and me of a breaking into their house. The doorframe was splintered badly. That was a bunch of bogus. We lived 20 miles away and didn't have a way to get to Lexton.

We boys spent every second weekend with Mom at Ron's farm close to the Vela Bridge by Redding. We loved going there. As we didn't have the experience of living in the country, there was a whole new way of life to explore.

Ron's 10 year old son, Jake, became our friend. He had light brown hair and big, blue eyes like swimming pools. He seemed a bit shy but actually did fit in well with our antics.

Ron taught us how to shoot with a bow and arrow into the bushes. We also learned target practice with rifles shooting tin soup cans sitting on fence posts. Trent had a very accurate aim and knocked lots of cans off the fence posts.

Mom had a maroone 1976 Pontiac Parisienne car that had been in an accident and was of little use to her. She let us drive the car through the small trails in the bush. After we boys got bored with driving the car (it was very dented and scratched by then), we decided to take our BB guns and fire holes into the car body. Mom asked why we would do such a crazy thing afterwards, but by the time she saw the car it was too late to reverse our actions. I mean, all us boys cared about was the fun of it.

Mom had a curly haired, black dog called "Misty" that she taught tricks. Basically Misty was a dumb animal, but after repeating and repeating instructions, Misty finally did roll over, sit and shake a paw.

Misty-First Pet

A dog house for "Misty" 1988

◆◆◆◆◆◆

Mom: I was cleaning house when I got the phone call from Lindsey Compton, Warren's sister. Her voice was shaking. "Warren died" she sobbed. What was she talking about?

Warren had a coffee in his hand and was driving his dad's big white van. He was up late with friends the night before. It was assumed he was sleepy and lost control of the van.

Chad: Mom phoned me at work and told me to sit down. Warren died that morning. My God! Why? I was stunned! This couldn't be real.

Jan (my girlfriend) came with me to Gerry and Rita's to pay our condolences. Gerry asked me to be a pallbearer. It was so hard to go to the funeral home and see my best friend just lying there, so white and waxy looking. Jan and I sat on a wooden bench in the entrance and Jan cradled me while I wept in her arms. I was devastated. I would miss Warren so much.

◆◆◆◆◆◆

Mom: In 1990 when Chad dated Jan, he seemed to be straightening out. It was probably the best time of his life, dating Jan and playing his guitar with his close friend, Shane. Paul thought it was cool to hang out with his brother then.

Chad:

Tomorrow

Tomorrow knows nothing more than what today has left undone

Tomorrow is a dream looking for a place to happen

Tomorrow is but the composure of a face that never lies

Tomorrow is but the extension of a loved one's smile

Tomorrow holds the key to the worlds of wonder and surprise

Tomorrow is the feeling something new is on the horizon

Tomorrow brings curious light to yesterday's darkness

Tomorrow is the shadow of what we do today.

◆◆◆◆◆◆

On my first date with Jan, we went to a cozy, little, affordable restaurant on the south side of the city. I remember her watching what food at I chose to eat. I was always planning what to eat ahead of time. I was very careful to try not to upset my stomach. I was flabbergasted by how much food Jan could wolf down, though!

I loved preparing breakfast for us on Sunday mornings. Mom had taught me how to cook eggs and toast when I was only five years old. After spending the day visiting with friends we returned back to the apartment. In the evening we worked on our homework together. When Jan asked for my opinion of one of her essays, she wouldn't agree with the answer that I gave her. Let's talk about positive criticism!

I picked on Jan a great deal. When I asked her to do something she wouldn't listen. Jan had a different way of doing things. We landed up fighting a lot. I guess it was mostly my fault (but not all...give me a break).

Jan and I went to a bar to listen to one of my favourite singers, Desiree. When Desiree and I were in high school together she gave me a CD of her music. Jan couldn't comprehend why we were at that bar in the first place. I suppose it was a warped idea to present my former favourite girlfriend to my present one.

Doug, (Jan's future boyfriend) and I used to write songs together. The deal was that the two of us would throw ideas back and forth. When I had a suggestion, I wanted the idea to be used. No one could make it any different. If Doug didn't want to play the music the way I thought it should be, then I would play it my way. Doug finally gave up on me, but we remained friends.

FRIENDS

In Cardelle I met Adam. We had a few things in common. We had weird stepfathers. We both strived to be on top. Adam only attended Brookside Composite High School with me for one year and decided to drop out. It was unfortunate. I was keen about graduating together.

Adam and I had memories. After Jake (another friend) and I had a fight, I decided not to give my buddies, Adam and Jake a ride home. Jake was so pissed that he knocked out the small right rear window of my car and cracked the windshield. I saw purple! Nobody was going to wreck my car and get away with it! I took a baseball bat and smashed Jake's windshield. Needles to say, Jake and I never spoke again.

People never knew what I was going to do next. In 1990 I worked at Tire Town. I began to feel paranoid. I felt that the guys I worked with were setting me up to be fired. I was accused of stealing from them and I really had no idea what they were talking about (at that time).

Later on I did need some tires for my car. Since I worked at Tire Town, I figured I could snag some. It was in the middle of the night. I had access to the entrance alarm system. I tiptoed into the shop and found four tires that would replace the worn tires on 1980 black Chrysler. I managed to roll the tires out of the shop into the back seat of my car and covered them with an old blanket. Once I arrived back at home I set the tires in the garage, intending to install them early the next morning.

My plan backfired, though. Somehow the owner found out and I had to appear in court for stealing. What was I thinking?

Being my first offence, I was assigned community hours...mostly working my punishment hours for the food bank, stocking shelves.

I worked in a convenience store for awhile after that. I managed to stay on track and was a first-rate employee. If truth be told, I did work very hard at whatever task was assigned to me.

For about a year I owned a red 1983 Farrago motor-cycle. Adam and I went for many rides. Adam was petrified when we soared over a set of tracks on 17th Street. He thought we were both going to plummet over the handlebars. I used to lay the bike down sideways, until we finally did wipe out. We were scraped up and the Motorcycle was a write-off.

Paul and I intended to take a road trip to the Oka-nogan on our motorcycles. By the time we reached Red-bowe, Paul didn't feel like riding anymore. We set off to Esmerald's for a beer. After more beers than necessary, we rolled out the sleeping bags under the trees at Rotterie Park. We awakened in about five hours to a vicious storm. Our beds were a sopping wet, cold mass of padding. Hopping onto our bikes as fast as we could pack things up, we sped back to Cardelle.

◆◆◆◆◆◆

Mom: I moved into Cardelle. He tried to make a good impression on me for that first six months we dated. Once I moved in with him, Ron turned out to be a colossal drunk. That was really unfortunate. Paul, Chad and Trent loved to visit the farm Ron and I had lived on. I left Ron.

The boys came to have Christmas back in Cardelle with me, in my small south side apartment. We found room in the corner of the living room for an artificial tree to decorate. I was happy again and my sons all seemed to be well adjusted.

I accompanied Chad to the Second Cup coffee shop a few times to watch him play guitar with Shane. Shane's band played basically Celtic music.

Chad's friends, whom I was sitting with, voiced their admiration for his talent. I was so proud of my son. The only music that Chad played that I recognized was a tune from my younger days "Johnny B Goode."

Chad: When Shane asked me to play guitar with him at the Second Cup, I preferred to substitute the Celtic tunes with faster, headier stuff. That was a real turn on for me, especially when Sheila, a friend of mine was there to listen.

Shane and I were teaming with ambition. We wrote songs together. I would format the song; Shane did the rhythm. He hoped to record and market the jazz songs in tribute of our friendship. We struggled to get back to the task over and over again, but other things seemed to keep getting in the way.

I was into philosophy. No one except Shane wanted to partake of my deep conversations about life. Here are a few a my thoughts:

Life wasn't handed down on a silver platter. Nature was more powerful than man was. We are but butt naked children in the forest of our dreams (we don't have the right to make a life and parade ourselves with achievements and material things, because who we are is seen...that's where we have to live at that point).

"Shane, please do not stay in one place (state of mind), and don't lose yourself or your dreams. Be as much yourself as you can" I advised him.

Shane and I lived together for awhile. I took Shane for a ride on my motorcycle. Shane had both our guitars on his back. We sped over to the Rocket bar in West Cardelle to have a few drinks (or more). We bought drinks for some chicks that came over to our table. Trying to be a smart-ass, Shane leaned against the wall and pulled the fire alarm. Someone saw Shane pull the alarm and the bouncer threw him into a corner.

"I'm out of here." I burst out. I wanted no part of the consequences. I took off as I heard fire trucks arriving. Shane was charged and presented with a fine. I did stay awake though, and returned to the bar after it was all over, to pick Shane up.

From about 15 to 18 years old, I had a bad collection of friends. Shane had a grudge against some of my friends. I can understand that. They got me to drop a very potent psychological drug. People were able to manipulate me because of my drug-induced state. If it wasn't for the fact I was always broke, one of my friends might have turned me into a coke addict.

About 1:00 am I hammered on the door at Dad's. Gail (my stepsister) answered the door. She was still living at home. "Please help me, I don't know what to do."

Because of being heavily stoned on mushrooms, I was in another world and grasping for reality. Gail took me to the Royal Mary Hospital emergency where my stomach was pumped. Having my stomach pumped was painful but somehow I knew I had to succumb to that kind of treatment or risk death.

BROOKSIDE COMPOSITE HIGH SCHOOL

Chad: Our crowd would have bush parties. I was pretty much the facilitator. That meant keeping the bonfire steadily blazing. I mingled to make sure people had somewhere to sit and knew where to find food and/or something to drink. It was important to me that everyone was having fun.

Up until 1991, I continued the rest of my education at Brookside Composite High School. It was a school for the arts. I received the Grade 11 Minor Award for the Highest Academic Average. My English teacher, Mr. Ross Harris, was my favourite teacher. Unfortunately he passed away a few years later.

Now this was cool. In 1990 our school presented a live theatre show called "Soundscapes." I was really pumped up about being on stage. I was beaming with pride as my parents watched from the audience.

A few years later I was the technical manager, a big part of the performance, "Godspell." It was a musical production about Jesus materializing in a subway background among conventional New Yorkers.

The most memorable occasion was our production of

"West Side Story." The story delves into the hostility between two rival gangs of different and cultural backgrounds in Manhattan's upper Westside and is reminiscent of Romeo and Juliet.

I was lucky enough to practice with Desiree, the beautiful girl who sang at that bar I took Jan to before. She had long, black, curly hair and an awesome smile. I saw the sparkle in her eyes as we talked, and my heart did flip-flop's. She sang like an angel, too. I was in love! During the performance I pointed out Desiree to Mom. "Mom, that's the girl I'm going to marry!"

Mom whispered that I had good taste in women.

I wrote this poem for Desiree:

The Spirit Guide

Voices in my head offer freedom to the slaves of circumstance

Strangers, like the fall of the ever-changing seasons, come faithfully to the dance

The Spirit Guide is calling from the darkness of consequence

The Spirit Guide brings flickering light to dreams of hopelessness

Where the voices turn from screams to whispers, and choices from wonder to hope, there stands the Spirit Guide

Like stars connected in nights of azure, she feeds on the powers of my soul

An angel sent from my despair; forever the Spirit Guide.

To Desiree
Love, Chad

There was a huge lunch of delicious desserts, coffee, tea and juice served after the concert.

◆◆◆◆◆◆

Mom: Chad was now six feet tall, with a trim build. He had dark brown hair and such big brown eyes. He was a handsome, popular young man. It was April 16, 1991. That evening I watched Chad play his guitar and sing at "West Side Story." I was so impressed! I didn't realize that Chad had so much talent. He even played the flute with the orchestra. I didn't even know he could play the flute! Later I found out he could play the piano, too. There was so much of his life that I missed when he moved in with his dad. Chad had inherited his Grandpa's gift of music.

Chad: Our crowd hung out at Dick's Pub on the West End. We partied at Dad's house a lot. Our house was like a train station. I played heavy metal with a friend, Joel. So many friends and friends of friends, dropped in. I tried to keep tabs on who came in and out of the house. That was an unpleasant task.

I had lost a total of three guitars from home, obviously stolen from our unknown guests. It was useless to report the thefts to the insurance company. What would they believe...one guitar missing, but three?

Paul saw a guitar with pedals at a garage sale some time later on. Was it mine? We'll never know.

Dad spent time between his job and his favourite pastime, the horse races. He sure got excited when he won money at the races. He would slip me money so I could go out with my friends. I didn't mind the "double your pleasure, double your fun" boomerang effect of his winnings.

Trent was home most of the time. Paul was usually out doing something with his friends.

GRADUATION

Chad: Life was once defined as a series of cycles or changes. With the hands of time we can experience a change every new day. Some things change slowly, like the changing color of leaves as our world whirls its way into a new season. People also change, whether it is physically or mentally. It is often so insignificant that we may never know the difference. On the other hand, it may also be so defined it can change our whole perspective to that person.

Time was flying by. It was my Grade 12 graduation day, June 5, 1991. This was it, the formal graduation ceremony at the end of 12 years...monkey suit and all. Mom and Dad were with me. Grandpa Stephen drove all the way here from the farm in Saskatchewan.

I decided to grow a moustache. The moustache was dark brown, like my hair and very parse, but it was a change.

Jan was my date. She wore a pale pink, satiny; spaghetti strapped dress, adorned with lace over the bodice, accessorized with long, pink gloves and spike heels. Jan looked gorgeous.

Chad

◆◆◆◆◆◆

Mom and Chad

◆◆◆◆◆◆

It was first-rate to be able to graduate together. I wore the customary red cap with the white tassel hanging over my eyes. Finally it was my turn. There were about 200 students graduating that day. I was the 141st. student to step onto the stage. The ceremony dragged on so long. As we each took our turns, Mr. Codel, the principal, took the cap tassel out of our eyes. I received my graduation scroll. I also received an Industrial Arts Award Certificate at the ceremony. I breathed the biggest sigh of relief that I can remember. I was thinking "Ha, ha! Later dates." This is the end of tedious school.

I was really nervous at the reception. I had arranged and narrated a slide show of some different goofy pranks and events that had happened during high school. I pulled it off! Whew, am I glad that's over. I could tell my family was very proud of me.

We grads were bussed into a high fenced yard on the north end of Cardelle. Now I can party and party and party! Adam joined us at the graduation party.

◆◆◆◆◆◆

After high school I just seemed to lose it. Any plans I had made for the future kept falling apart. Nothing panned out for me. I didn't want to land up like some other people I knew, who subsisted in poverty.

I had to find a place to reside because Dad had sold his house and moved in with his lady friend, Jean. That's when Adam and I shared a condo owned by Dad in the Westrose area. It was a main floor condo. We had very little furniture, but it was the first home of our own and we had to start somewhere. By browsing the second hand stores, we found a couple of mattresses to sleep on, a small card table and two wooden chairs. That was it for now.

Adam and I were hired for our first jobs after high school, working at Universal Furniture as salesmen. In no time at all we had managed to save enough money to each purchase a car, within two weeks of each other. I bought a black Olds. Adam bought a Honda Prevue. His car turned out to be a $2000 lemon.

A lot of partying went on during those years. We were having a few drinks and cruising around on the south side of Cardelle. My car slid off the road and stalled. We just ditched the car and ran off. Isn't it amazing, what power a few drinks can have?

Adam and I didn't get along as roommates, so he moved out of the condo. We decided not to live together again, in order to preserve our friendship.

DIRECTION

Chad: I needed some direction in my life. I wasn't sure what. I wanted to be respected by being somebody. Jean said that I could easily have excelled in broadcasting, music or writing. Those were unquestionably my best talents. Something inside me wanted to help other people with their mental and emotional problems. I felt that would make my life more rewarding.

In 1993 I decided to enroll at North Side Academy. I had grandiose dreams of obtaining a Bachelor of Arts Degree in Psychology. I maintained First Class Standing in my grades.

I was in my second year of college when I contracted mononucleosis. In six weeks I landed up in emergency at the Royal Mary Hospital. I was treated for intestinal pain and immediately discharged. I lay on Mom's couch day after day for six months. It took that long for the mononucleosis to disappear and then intestinal pain developed.

My dream came to a halt. I decided to drop out of college. After one and a half years of struggling, sick and broke, there just didn't seem to be any point to continuing. Even though I had another student loan for college, who wanted to be saddled with more loans that I had to pay back for eight years and not be certain of a job afterwards?

In 1990 I set off to live my live with Mom and Brett (her common-law husband) in their Langercourt town home.

During that time I invented an environmental garbage disposal product. My Mom and Brett thought it was a great product and agreed to help me finance the patenting and marketing of the disposal unit. We interacted with a patenting company in the U.S. Mom took $5000 out of her RRSP's for this venture. Through correspondence and phone calls back and forth to the U.S., we finally realized the patent company was a scam. There was no recourse for us except to try and put together a class action suit against the patenting company. It would have taken up too much of Mom's time to pursue this as she was still working full time at a long term nursing care institution. We learned a lesson...to never do business with anyone you can't see face to face.

Mom and I commenced singing lessons in the evenings at North Side Academy. I really enjoyed the classes in spite of the fact that the pianist seemed to be playing for herself, not the individual students. As the voice teacher was going over theory in the classroom, each one of us was sent in turn to a small piano studio to review our chosen song music with the pianist. Not only did the pianist not get my composition arrangement the way that I wanted but also I missed out on the theory taught back in class. I was a perfectionist and my music had to be precise. It was so frustrating.

Mom, Dad and Grandpa came to the recital. I was so anxious. I was dreadfully sick that night. The wrenching abdominal pain affected my performance. My first song was "Stairway to Heaven" by Eric Clapton. I started out feeble. Between my illness and the nervousness that took over my whole being, the first selection came out as a quiet croak. As I persisted, my confidence increased. Dad was astonished "you really can sing!"

Mom preferred not to sing at the recital. Our voices were taped on a cassette recorder in class and she felt her voice would annoy everyone. Stage fright would have got the best of Mom's singing anyway. At least she realized before it was too late.

Mom: For about a year Chad lived in a West Cardelle basement suite in a small stucco house that a fellow named Jim owned. Chad had a tall and blonde lady friend, Cheryl. Cheryl had a little girl, Barbie. Chad became very attached to both of them, although Cheryl didn't have the same feelings for him. When Cheryl needed a sitter, he babysat Barbie for Cheryl anyway.

Chad was like that. He was very thoughtful of others wants and feelings. There was a time Paul commented that he liked Chad's shoes, so Chad gave the shoes to him. Whenever my birthday or Christmas came up, he always gave me a memorable gift. He gave me an expertly framed painted Easter egg with a poem written on it. Another gift I received was a plaque that said "Mother" on it and had room for my photo. They were always gifts that came from the heart.

I was in between moves and needed to crash at Chad's. I slept on the pullout couch for a few days. It wasn't very comfortable; a few springs were poking out, but at least I was with my son. I was shocked (like most moms) at how dirty the shower was. Chad was such a perfectionist; I never dreamed that his home would be anything less than immaculate, so why the grime?

Jim was working out of town. Even though Jim was so good to him, Chad went into Jim's kitchen cupboards and helped himself to cleaning products. I guess Chad thought that he could manage to buy his other provisions but when it came to cleaning, someone else's would have to do. I don't know why he left that basement suite. Maybe Jim found out, or maybe Chad couldn't afford the rent anymore. Jim even brought Chad's mail to Ralph's after he moved out of the basement.

◆◆◆◆◆◆

Chad systematically swallowed pills, three at a time, until the bottle was empty. In a while he phoned Trent and Trent phoned Ralph. They rushed over to Chad's but the ambulance had already taken him to the Royal Mary Hospital. The doctor wouldn't allow visitors. This may have been his first suicide attempt.

Chad: My thoughts went through a journey of discovery and enlightenment; we are limitless and boundless, yet, often we seem confined by that which defines us...that which has no meaning.

It seems as though more often than not these days, I will catch myself in what seems like a profound state of introspection. For instance, even now as I sit here writing, some part of me feels as if I'm elsewhere. That is, not to imply that somewhere along the way I became less the man than my 26 years might suggest. However, I can no longer deny that I feel as if I'm in what can only be described as sort of ongoing state of deja vu. Although this would tend to be something some might consider the manifestation of a troubled mind. I have come to know it more as a gentle reminder that we grow and evolve only with an awareness of ourselves. An awareness of why at one moment we may tend to feel somewhat lost, while in another it's as if we are indeed precisely where it is we are supposed to be.

It is only with certain contemplation that I conclude for my own purposes that time is in a sense of a scale, each moment a point of changing balance between everything previous and anything we anticipate. Ironically, however, at best it has been the case for me that as the plot thickens, each page adds more consequence to the next and as I would naturally follow, the page I am on at any given moment always finds me wondering what shall come. Yet, as it stands, I'm finding it's more sensible to read each one page at a time without neither expectation nor regret.

From this moment on, all I can hope for is that if I'm honest with myself that perhaps every moment can be filled with the conscious reminder that I truly am alive and well. So, let the scales measure that our true desire must be to see with our hearts what minds often deny.

◆◆◆◆◆◆

That's about the same time I hacked off my ponytail. It was time to become a man. I decided to use my practical skills on massage therapy. I had business cards printed with my company name on them. At this time I was residing in a room at the Mayfair Hotel. My room became my clinic.

HCC INDEPENDENT THERAPIES

Chad Stephen
**Massage and Nutritional
Counselling Specialist**

Lowest Rate • MB Guarantee

Mayfair Apts.	Tel: (780) 423-1650
10815 - Jasper Avenue	Room # 107 For Appointment
Edmonton Alberta.	(Leave Message)

Well, that was a colossal waste of time and effort. There were no calls for my services. After all, who would come to a strange man's hotel room for a massage? I paced the floor for lack of having something meaningful to do. Day after day, I waited for something to happen. The only client I had was an older lady I had met in the hospital, even before setting up my clinic.

With the renewal of my faith I began to look for spiritual healing. I was at St. Bastil's Church. Surprisingly, I spotted a lady I knew and tapped her on the shoulder. It was Rita, Warren's mother. I told her of my quest for spiritual healing. I was trying desperately to find any solution to ease me of my pain and grief. Rita knew where there was a healing service and asked if I cared to join her there. The healing service calmed me down but didn't accomplish any miraculous healing.

Rita understood I had nowhere to live. She offered me accommodation in her and Gerry's home. I felt so comfortable...so comfortable that I took liberties that a son would in his own parents' home. Me, not realizing how my actions would affect others, ran their phone bill up $37 on a telephone dating service. I had an obsession with finding the perfect mate. Who would want an unstable man anyway? Unfortunately, I never could repay them for that phone bill.

THE SPIRAL

Chad: I began going from doctor to doctor searching for a real diagnosis for my pain. Mom's doctor claimed it was" Irritable Bowel Syndrome". La de da. What's that...a name for what doctors' don't have knowledge of? Another doctor reflected that my illness might be Chronic Fatigue Syndrome. I endured a battery of exploratory exams. None of the doctors could pinpoint the origin of my intestinal pain.

Dr. Lesniuk, a naturopathic, took a live blood cell analysis and diagnosed me with Candidadiasis. Homeopathic herbs, vitamins, and acupressure were prescribed. I felt terrible for two weeks (the cleansing of my colon was occurring). For the next two weeks I was free from pain and elated, until the pain commenced again. I couldn't afford to return to Dr. Lesniuk for further treatment because the treatments were not covered by my health insurance plan. Later, when I accumulated some more money, I visited Dr. Palabar. He did the live blood cell analysis twice over time and also diagnosed me with Candidadiasis.

I went to see a gastroentologist, Dr. Contic, at the Royal Mary Hospital. More tests were completed. Those tests showed unexplained inflammation of the bowel. I was prescribed an anti-inflammatory medication, which didn't ease the pain at all. I kept changing my diet in hopes of finding a miracle solution.

Mom: Chad's friends gradually vanished because all Chad could talk about was the state of his intestinal pain and his latest diet. Adam stuck by him as best he could. They were friends for 13 years. Trent and Adam would visit Chad in the hospital. It would be a familiar sight to see Chad in his blue, open-backed hospital gown, eating grapes.

This began the deterioration of a super intelligent, talented and envied young man. My son's life was gradually disintegrating before my eyes.

The transfer of patients with Candidadiasis to psychiatric care is common. When the doctors don't identify or understand Candidadiasis, psychiatry seems to be a "wise" solution.

Chad: The doctors didn't really recognize what was wrong with me. Existing in a psychiatric ward was like being in a prison of insanity with nowhere or no one to turn to. The only psychiatric problem I had is the continuous frustration of constant intestinal pain and nobody believing me.

Next, I decided to try a hospital out of town. I was admitted to the psychiatric ward at the Rock Valley Hospital. I remained there for about six months. The doctors felt the pain was pseudo-symptomatic, meaning it was "all in my head." Didn't they get it? My head was two and a half feet from my intestines!

Then I met Dr. Wesley at the Rock Valley Hospital. He not only attempted over and over again to be of assistance to me, but also took the time to research Candidadiasis.

Dr. Wesley did spiritual counselling with me. We would read the bible, looking for comforting messages symbolizing a new future. At last my faith was being restored. I relied on God's words and Dr. Wesley's help for almost a year.

Dr. Wesley helped me perceive a brighter future and gave me reason to say thank you, God, for my life. I presented Dr. Wesley with a silver cross on a chain for Christmas that year.

Paul thought it was strange that I would pray with a doctor. What difference did it make to anyone else? I had to survive the best way I could.

Through contemplation I came to the conclusion that I should start making plans for my new lease on life, knowing that I could be well again. Up until now I've just put my life on hold because I wasn't sure if I had a future. Now, however, I reckon I ought to just live like the future is picture perfect and let the pieces fall where they may.

SHOCK THERAPY

Mom: There is a family history of depression. My cousin hung himself. Chad's cousin and two uncles are unable to care for themselves, living an empty life and dependant on their parents for sustenance. His grandmother and aunt both had deep depression and mental challenges.

Chad phoned me just about every night talking suicide for the last two or three years. I would attempt to calm him down to the point of making it through the night. I advised him to call a psychiatrist or the distress line and he would usually call the distress line. Then he was able to function for awhile again.

I wonder now, if at that time, God was preparing to call Chad home. Chad compiled his will over and over again. He composed poetry based on angels and heaven.

If I didn't hear from Chad even one day, I would hop into my car and frantically search for him, wherever I thought he might be. I really never knew what condition I would find my son in. My existence had been put on a roller coaster. This erratic routine between us was upsetting my life. I revolved around his needs. Yet, this wasn't a situation in which to exercise tough love.

Chad: In the end I landed up in the North Side Hospital. I

was in and out of that hospital for approximately nine months. The doctors weren't accomplishing anything. I was weary of being drugged up and waiting until they determined what to do with me next. Every time I turned around it seemed that there was a new innovative and improved drug to disguise my pain. I felt like a guinea pig.

When there was a break in my treatment plan, I became restless and just disgusted with the whole process. I decided to shatter the fire hose window to obtain a piece of glass. Then I sneaked to my room and slit my wrists. Of course the nurse discovered me laying on my bed, bleeding and waiting to end all of this torment. I should have realized that the staff would catch me. I was lethargic and in recurrent states of anxiety and so, so fatigued. I just wanted to hibernate here and not remember the outside world.

At last Dr. Seare administered 24 shock treatments to me in a five-day span. After the treatments I felt fantastic. I even believed there was nothing wrong with my colon after all. My memory was no damn good, but I didn't worry. There was nothing significant in my life that I felt I had to recall; I could pretend I was someone else, who never had a care in the world!

Then again the memory loss may have been a symptom of my former Candidadiasis. I stopped speaking about getting well, just about being discharged from the hospital.

Mom: Shock treatments are supposed to be safe. I was around my son more than anyone else was. As a licensed practical nurse I had the capacity to notice the objective signs of his condition. Chad did lose parts of his memory. Chad forgot where his room was in the hospital. He didn't know what he was doing. He failed to remember situations that had happened before in his life.

Chad did a lot of reading so he felt he was always

one up on Dr. Seare's instructions and would only follow the instructions until he thought there was no medical purpose for the treatments. This meant going on and off the psychiatric mediations. It would have a disastrous effect on his mental and emotional stability.

Adam and I were discussing Chad's behaviour. Adam had been taking a psychology class at the time. His professor felt Chad's brain was generalizing the pain. Hypochondria came to mind as a possibility, too.

Adam and I felt that ninety per cent of Chad's illness was probably due to the drug cocktails being administered to him. It sucks. I didn't have any confidence in the treatments being administered to Chad. The manuals the doctors used to diagnose by seemed to be only theory. Each person's body is so diverse and unique, so why wouldn't Chad need an individual treatment plan?

Chad: I struggled to get more financial aid from Social Services by forging a letter, supposedly from my doctor. Social Services phoned Dr. Seare, whereas the doctor decided to help me, instead of going against me.

Dr. Seare assisted in applying for Assured Income for the Severely Handicapped funding for me to survive on. Even with this steady income, I still didn't have sufficient money for the specialty yeast free foods and herbal supplements I required.

Mom: Grandpa Stephen provided money to Chad frequently. It seemed whatever Chad wanted from Grandpa, he got.

Chad's dad had lent him his credit card. Chad visited the casino. There was a special machine that didn't ask for a PIN number. He phoned in his dad's card number to accumulate a tidy sum of $600.00.

ON THE MOVE

Chad: After I left the North Side Hospital I moved in with Trent. This move didn't pan out as expected. I wanted everything to be orderly and in sequence. Trent was more laid back and left a trail of mess wherever he went.

Then I camped at Dad's. I incessantly borrowed money from Dad to get my darn student loan paid off. Plus, I required extra money for groceries and medicines. Dad appeared to be the only person who could help me out financially. I was always apprehensive about asking him for assistance. My Dad was annoyed with me a lot. He preached to me but I wouldn't listen.

Dad was always inviting me to go places with Jean and him but I refused. Dad and Jean went to Grandpa's funeral in 1996. I was supposed to drive Dad's truck to Saskatchewan. I didn't even go. I couldn't face the loss of my Grandpa Stephen. Also, there would be an immense spread of food afterwards, which, if I ate, would only make me feel sicker. Paul and Trent went with the car. Mom went to the funeral, too, unexpectedly. She loved the old guy like a father.

◆◆◆◆◆◆

Dad and Jean discovered that there was a forced entry into their home when they were gone. The cupboard and dresser drawers were in disorder. Jean's heirloom jewellery and Dad's old money were missing. A laptop computer, camera, radio and facsimile machine had vanished. Tools and sports equipment were gone. It was assumed I was the thief, because the dog (Bear) would have raised a ruckus if a stranger had tried to break into the house. It had to be an inside member of the family.

The sports equipment was found in my car. I don't know what to say. Was I so round the bend that I had to upset Dad and Jean? Did I pawn most of the things for cash? By that time I was so mentally confused, I didn't even remember that the robbery happened. Was I overly medicated? Was I the guilty one or not?

I sure didn't appreciate others admonishing me about what I ate. Because of my disease of Candidadiasis, I refused to eat with the family. I wouldn't sit back and take it.

"What do you think I've been reading for the last two years? After all, I had a year and a half of psychology under my belt, even though we younger people know it all!" Meals turned into a fiasco, so exit left was my easiest option.

Problems developed because of the disbelief that Candidadiasis was an actual disease. Dad and my brothers became very exasperated with my illness and me. They absolutely refused to discuss "the "disease. They all believed that my suicide threats were just pleas for attention. Yes, I needed attention. I couldn't seem to find a solution and I didn't know what the answer would be. I was so bewildered most of the time. My family became distant towards me.

Mom: Chad returned home to me. I couldn't afford to

provide for my own son. The stress of his illness was exhausting for me.

Chad was 25 years old this year. I issued him an ultimatum. He had to locate his own residence by the end of January 2000. From now on I would only permit him to reside with me for a few days at a time. It was time to try "tough love," even if I didn't feel comfortable with the idea. I felt this would help Chad become more responsible for himself.

Chad tried to exist on his own. My principal mistake was helping him obtain a bankcard. He was able to get a bankcard by giving the bank a $100 security deposit. He forever ran the card to the hilt buying things he couldn't afford. He purchased guitars and stereo equipment that later on he turned around and pawned for cash.

Chad: I depleted a lot of my monthly AISH cheque on drugs. It's no wonder I resorted to pilfering for rent and groceries. I had to live somehow.

Companionship Brings Hope

Chad:

Together

Together we laugh like angels on a cloud

Together we fall like the comet without a landing

We chase the moon like spacemen strong and proud.

Once I was alone like the silence of the trees standing

Together is the chance we take to be held without some longing

Perhaps together isn't always a condition of the heart.

◆◆◆◆◆◆

Mom: Chad sought after a job, wife and children. Most of his friends were married and already had one or two children.

He did eventually find a girlfriend, Dalice, who stuck by him for about a year. It was a relationship of two people drowning in each other's depression.

Chad: I was anxious to meet the right woman; she would be the love of my life. Was I grasping at straws? If so, would it be the last straw?

When I was congregating in a bar with my friends, I came upon Dalice, a very slender, aboriginal girl with long, black, shimmering hair. She was very timid and a loving, giving person. I grew to love Dalice very much.

In only two months we found a basement suite that we thought we could afford. It was such a wonderful feeling, going out and buying provisions for our mutual home. We had purchased a metal-framed double bed, a brown card table with two chairs and a couch that was still in good condition. We didn't have much in the way of kitchen supplies but Mom gave us whatever she could spare. Dalice decorated our suite with a dream catcher and decorative wall hangings.

Dalice shared almost everything with me, even extra money that she had received from her family. I bought her little things like makeup. We did what we could with the money we had.

We even had the brief thrill of expecting a baby. I telephoned my parents, longing to share my joy with them. Unfortunately, the pregnancy was a false alarm.

Dalice had a friend, Carol, who had four children. Penny was the third child. She was a four-year-old pixie with chin-length, raven-black hair.

Penny's mom admitted to us that she mistreated her child. Penny's siblings were nurtured adequately. Penny just happened to be in the family line-up where it seemed to be so problematical to treat her with the kindness and love that her siblings received. Carol, realizing that this was very wrong, appealed to Dalice and me to take Penny and raise her as our own.

We welcomed Penny with anticipation into our home. We purchased clothes and toys for her. We cuddled her continuously. Penny would sob "Mommy? Mommy? As hard as we tried to console her, she would not stop crying for her mom.

Dalice and I finally had no choice but to return Penny to her mom; she in turn handed the child over to her Grandmother to raise. Carol knew Penny would receive the care and love she deserved from her grandmother.

◆◆◆◆◆◆

"Don't you think it's time to iron our clothes?" I asked Dalice.

"I'll do the ironing after we come back from the store."

I screamed at Dalice that she was useless. All of a sudden I became violent. I broke a window and a chair in anger. What's wrong with me? This is not really me! The stupid prescribed drugs I was taking did a number on me. I beat Dalice up. She had a black cheek and a terribly sore ribcage, besides the destruction of her trust in me. Mom taught me to never, ever hit girls. What happened to that piece of insight? Even as I went berserk I knew, just knew my actions were all wrong.

Dalice and I fought on a regular basis. I was never happy with the way things were done. She knew how precise I was about things, but yet would still try to live with it. She would pull back, letting me do as I pleased, especially after that last outburst of violence from me.

Mom told me that our relationship would never work, because we were both suffering from depression, but I thought I could make our bond succeed anyway. We became engaged.

I was wrong. Dalice and I broke up many times. After we separated, she would phone me all day long, everyday. Eventually, I quit answering the phone.

Finally, Dalice and I broke up for good. I became isolated again.

STORY TO TELL

Chad: Trent now had a baby daughter. She was so cute and chubby. Victoria looked like a punk rocker, with her thick, pitch black hair standing on end all over her head.

This poem is dedicated to my niece, Victoria. To look into her eyes is to truly understand the power of an innocent love that I believe can transcend the boundaries of both this world and the next. If you ever wonder about the true meaning of life simply look into the eyes of a child to find purest form of a soul, untouched by the burdens of time and misfortune.

I Dream

I dream of things felt but untold in the night

I dream that flowers bloom in the heart of a child

Like the rain that slowly begins to fall,

Dreams flow into the recesses of my mind.

I dream that forever is the peace I've found in your eyes

I dream that all that is sacred holds me in the arms of eternal grace

Like the secrets that hold us softly between pleasure and pain,

Dreams follow me into the tender touch of your arms.

We are limitless and boundless,

Yet that which means nothing confines us.

There are things along the way, which will bring us solace and peace.

I dream of the wonders we will share with raindrops and tears.

◆◆◆◆◆◆

Mom: Chad's life was at a stand still. I kept encouraging him to write because I knew he had a story to tell, in expectation that he would accomplish something meaningful. Maybe this would present him with a new lease on life.

Chad: Paul never really spoke to me much when I was down. Anyway, we had nothing in common anymore. Paul would attempt to do something for me and somehow I would muddle it up. He felt I was "unbalanced". He said it made him ill to see what was happening to me.

When I threatened suicide, Paul yelled "Go ahead, kill yourself, but don't drag the whole family through years and years of this crap! Why are you trying to make the family's life so difficult? You're running the family through the mill and it's not fair."

Paul hesitantly decided he didn't want anything to do with me because he didn't have any control over the weird things I did. It hit me very hard. I felt like the whole world had exploded. I idolized my big brother so much, and now I had seemingly lost him. Everything glazed in front of me, as if I was on caffeine high and couldn't see straight or function.

By this time other symptoms of Candidadiasis had set

in. Confusion, anxiety and severe depression accompanied my intestinal pain.

I resorted to what other people thought was abusing my body. Experimentation with diets that I expected would cure or eradicate my intestinal pain became part of my existence. My ritual of drinking cabbage juice or water spiked with bleach was normal for me. For awhile, I would only consume beans. Yet, I was vulnerable like anyone else. Periodically, I fell back into binging on cookies, a pie or McDonald's food.

Mom: Chad's illness increased with intensity. There was a constant fixation on his colon. His depression intensified. His mental functioning became distorted. Chad knew how to do tasks but had trouble carrying through.

He subsisted in the Cromdale Hotel, in a rundown part of the city for a short time. A couple of his friends, who he knew well, conned money from him by promising him truck driving jobs. It would cost $600 for the training fee. Well, great friends! They walked away with the money and no explanation about how the training would transpire. Chad just kissed away his only income for the month.

◆◆◆◆◆◆

Chad:

The Things I Need

Where do I find the things I need?

Like an obscure dream, the things I need hold me in the silence of your eyes

Where do I find the things I need?

More often than not the things I need push and sway my soul between the extremes of lucidity and changing circumstance

The things I need leave me longing to know once again the love of a stranger

Where do I find the things I need?

My heart and my soul tell me often that the things I need are only as far as my mind will allow them to reach.

◆◆◆◆◆◆

Chad: I resided in a decrepit rooming house downtown on skid row with a new girlfriend, Jenny. I was so proud to have her in my life and bragged to Mom how impressed I was with Jenny's talent. She was very adept and creative at making crafts to sell at Farmers' Markets. Guess what? Most crafts don't sell. Between the two of us, we didn't have enough money to survive. Jenny had to leave me.

In my desolation and grief, I decided to swallow all the pills I could find. I started to mellow out. All of sudden, I felt weird sensations. I freaked out and started yelling at the top of my voice. I couldn't move off the bed. In terror, I screamed louder and louder.

Finally, somehow, one of my neighbours heard me in my suite, bust in the door and phoned the ambulance. As usual, I landed up in the Royal Mary Hospital emergency, getting my stomach pumped. It was a very painful procedure. I hated that, but the previous mental anguish always blocked the memory of stomach pumping out of my mind.

I was evicted from my suite because the management didn't want the police or ambulance there. It was bad for their business.

Psychiatric Ward

Chad:

In Dreamland

The plains of consciousness divided by night and day;

A residue of lingering hope falls to cover softly what the soul longs to hold

Thoughts held secret find place near the midnight hour.

The old friend for whom a love remains untold

Where the light breaks open what dark night conceals;

A mind then wonders what the new day reveals.

The plains of consciousness divided by streams of peacefulness

In dreamland our greatest desire finds certain validity.

Without a dream night is but a delve into temporary, silent lucidity.

◆◆◆◆◆◆

    I had nowhere to reside, so I returned to the home Dalice and I had shared. I knew the garage there was vacant. I still possessed a mattress in the back seat of my car. I hauled the mattress onto the dirt floor of the garage. For many days I slept in the garage. There was not a thing to keep me occupied, except a radio.

Oh, yes, I had my cell phone, too. That was operating on a phone card. When the card was depleted I wouldn't even be able to phone Mom and Dad for help. I was afraid to phone Dad too much. Begging for help was so degrading; especially when I had to beg so frequently. I would start to dial and then hang up.

This was the point of seclusion for me. It was too embarrassing to let my friends (the few I had left) know how I was living. How could I allow my friends or family to see me in this appalling situation. I felt they were unapproachable.

◆◆◆◆◆◆

There was no one left to shoot the breeze with. I felt wretched about my existence. I wasn't even a human being anymore. No one gave a damn about me, except Mom, and I didn't want to continually bother her. Once more, I ingested all the pills I could find. Then I got really panicky again. I meandered out into the back alley.

I regained consciousness in the hospital. The police said someone gave an account of a man passed out in the snow. The police called for an ambulance. Why in the hell didn't they let me give up the ghost?

The doctor and my family deliberated and decided that I should be in a group home, because I had trouble taking care of myself. It was like I had no brains left or something. It was easier to make everyone happy; I decided to make an attempt to live there.

It was a stucco house on the north side of the city, which had been converted into an institution. We each had our own bedrooms. The caregivers did try. They were polite and kind to all of us. It just wasn't what I needed. The group home was for real mentally challenged people. I was normal, compared to the other clients. I could have taken care of the clients myself.

Mom: I stopped in at the group home to visit Chad. I wanted to see how he was adjusting to the atmosphere. I could see that Chad was irritable and restless. He had a cherry-red rash all over his face and body. I had seen him with this type of rash many times. It usually meant his anxiety level was high. God please let him adjust! There is nowhere else for him to go that would be suitable and safe for him.

Chad: That effort only lasted one month. I left the group home. I left most of my belongings, as usual. I had prearranged a sale of my little black & white TV for a few bucks.

◆◆◆◆◆◆

Somehow my life kept exploding. I ran out of money because I considered it necessary to buy natural remedies from the health food store, instead of paying for rent and other provisions. That meant I had to establish another way to obtain food. The food bank would only permit so many orders a month per person. Even the food banks weren't available at night. After I exhausted that prospect, I found myself shopping for free, or to put it bluntly, shop lifting.

I was eventually apprehended by the police and transported to the Remand Centre. The guards placed me in a cell only four feet by six feet. I suffered like an animal. My illness reached an all time high. The prison wouldn't provide me the type of food that I needed to sooth my severe stomach pain. I was stripped of my herbs and supplements.

My nerves were on edge. I counted the dirt spots on

the concrete walls. I tried to create songs in my head. I tried to think of my childhood...anything to take my mind off the closed in walls and absence of stimulation.

It was the second day of my imprisonment. Unbelievably, today was my 27th birthday. Mom turned up to visit me, bringing a card and a homemade cake with white icing and an aqua edging. Mom wasn't allowed to give me the cake. She took the cake home and froze it until I was released. I wasn't even given the birthday card. Even when I was released from the Remand Centre, the card wasn't given to me. At least my Mom was allowed to stay and visit for 15 minutes. The guard had a good laugh beyond compare, on our heartbreak.

Shadows in the Mist

Subtle shadows in the mist are like dreams to be tasted

Pretending the soft voice of a loved one is at arm's length

Sometimes making believe that it was not lost in the wonder of it all

Acting like the evils of the world are nevermore our crosses to bear

Imaging what makes me whole is just being alive to see a new day's sun

Knowing that night moves into day

Will bring peace to hearts longing for contentment.

◆◆◆◆◆◆

Dr. Locke felt that I would benefit from psychiatric therapy. I was admitted to the Royal Mary Hospital again. I tell you, I will leave here if the doctor doesn't find a way to relieve this anxiety and intestinal pain this time. I'm so dog-tired of going through the incessant medication changes and withdrawals.

Sarah was a patient in the hospital with me. She appeared to have the same intestinal problem as mine. It makes me want to cry when I think that she may very well spend her life as she is. I often feel like reaching out to her somehow, but am afraid to because she seems so fragile. I can only pray that her life is tolerable.

I have to tell you, being in here is like being surrounded by little children. Some of them seem lost and others just seem infantile. It's like they are possessed in some way. Nonetheless, most of them have such child-like innocence about them. I don't know if I should pity or envy them.

Another thing I find unusual is that most of the patients here watch nothing but the news on the television. What's really strange is that they all seem to watch with such intensity; I have to wonder if they're not really trying to figure out what's going on in the outside world, or if it's going to end altogether.

THE PROCESS

Chad: I think I can honestly say that at present the one thing I can credit my mother for is that somewhere along the way she managed the values of hope and faith....the notion that life can be something to cherish whether you want it or not. As for my father, I can only say that I gained the inherent stubbornness to never give up despite the influence of any circumstance. Yet, though these things often seemed as if they were expected of me, more so than given as guidelines by which to carry myself; I am truly thankful that they remain part of me. I know that it is due also in part to a responsibility they did not take lightly.

My resources were so lacking; I didn't know what my next step was. I asked Trent if I could make an attempt to live with him once more. He was living in a small house on the north side of Cardelle and now that Victoria, his baby daughter was in his life, expenses added up. Trent appreciated having a roommate to help out. It seemed Trent and I were fighting all the time. I required things to be just so...a clean house and only particular people allowed to visit. I realize a lot the disagreements we had were my own fault.

In early May of 2000, some friends of Trent's came by to visit. After they left, Trent was told that $900 had been stolen from one of his friends. There was also a female drug addict there that day. Trent accused me of pocketing the money. Trent and I got into a real physical brawl. The toilet was broken and blood was splattered all over the place.

Trent demanded that the $900 be returned because it was his friend's only source of income. I tell you, it wasn't me this time. There were other people in the house who could have filched the money as well. In the end, Trent opted to stay at a friend's home for the night. We both needed time to cool down and assess the situation.

Later, Trent told the drug addict and me that the garage would be unlocked for the night and the money could be returned at that time, with no questions asked.

The next day the $900 was found in the garage and the issue was closed. I will never forget how deeply insulted I was.

◆◆◆◆◆◆

Trent was out doing errands. I was home by myself, stewing in my own brew. I mean literally drowning myself in booze to the hilt. Sometime during the night, I phoned Dad, not being capable of talking coherently. Dad just instructed me to sleep it off. I slurred "OK".

The whole world was pissing me off. Everyone was frustrated with me. No one understood anything I said. Nobody was concerned about my welfare. That's it, I'll give them something to think about.

I stumbled downstairs to the furnace and blew out the pilot light. I staggered back into the living room to drink some more. I waited.

No! No! Yeah, I panicked again. Suddenly afraid for my life, I phoned an ambulance. The police were alerted. Police cars swarmed all over the place. The whole block was evacuated for protection against a potential explosion.

This was a lot more serious than I thought! The story of my escapade was written up in the local newspaper.

All at once it was like a bucket of water thrown in my face. Reality hit home. I was in profound trouble. I was transported back to the loony bin at the Royal Mary Hospital....with a security guard scrutinizing my every move.

◆◆◆◆◆◆

Mom: Chad was unable to make his money stretch to cover his basic living expenses. At times he was short on rent. He existed in a garage, sometimes in his car, or tried to bunk at a homeless shelter. Many times the shelter would be full. The shelter's staff couldn't supply his special diet. During the day the clients were required to go out on the street. The shelters were only meant for overnight accommodation. Being outside was supposed to give we clients a chance to formulate a change in their lives. Even in the freezing, bitter winter we were forced outside.

The odd time he would be able to rent a seedy hotel room. One time he left his hotel room to enjoy some fresh air. A hooker or drug addict broke into his room and stole a month's rent. Chad couldn't believe that his acquaintances would steal from him. He had hung out with these people for awhile now.

A man in the hotel ventured into the hallway of the hotel, saw Chad and assumed he was a police officer. He became aggressive and threatened to kill Chad.

In breathless fear, my son tore down the hallway into his own room and phoned me. I told him to leave there as fast as he could. I was living in a newer area on south side. I instructed him to join me in my two bedroom walk-out basement suite until he could locate suitable accommodation elsewhere.

Chad had been on a suicide mission. During the last eight years he overdosed about ten times. He slit his wrists twice. He attempted to hang himself with his belt. His belt broke. Chad told Adam that he had bought a white Toyota so he could gas himself. All he was missing was a hose. Adam just blew it off. Each attempt was always his "last time". He gave up on having a social life. He didn't feel like seeing anyone anymore.

◆◆◆◆◆◆

Chad:

Something Strange

There's a changed order on the things we take for granted

There's a difference between what's real and what's not

Something strange follows me into the darkness of that which can never be understood

In a night of certain silence there's usually nothing left to the imagination

There's a change of heart when the pieces of love and hope

Fall into the corners of an open mind

Something strange finds itself wanting for less than a soul in some state of deliverance

In light of all that's found me here with longing and abandon

Something strange won't let me be at ease

There's something strange in the things that leave us here

In this never ending state of conjecture.

◆◆◆◆◆◆

Mom: Chad was admitted to the Royal Mary Hospital on

May 23, 2000. This time security was tight, so that he would not hurt himself or others. I set out to visit Chad. I was distraught to see that things had become this extreme.

We both sat on the edge of the bed. I sat very close to my son. I was trying to comfort Chad as best as I was able. I enclosed him in my arms and rocked him. Would there ever be happiness and health for him? I could feel the anguish in his heart. I sensed at that moment that Chad had realized his future.

Chad: Dad came to visit me. It was pouring rain that day. I was overwhelmed. I didn't believe that he'd come to see me. I felt so warm and fuzzy. I was even chatting about getting well again. Dad presented me with $10.00 for coffee and other provisions. He begged me to phone him when I was ready to leave the hospital.

It would be the last time Dad set eyes on me. He returned to visit me once more at 1 pm, but missed me by about one hour.

◆◆◆◆◆◆

It was noon on June 9, 2000 when I discharged myself from the hospital. I spent $321of my sparse money on a black 1981 Ford Marquis car from a dealership on 82nd Avenue. I purchased a hose from Canadian Tire on Friday.

Mom: Ralph had queried the doctors about why Chad was discharged from the hospital, when it didn't seem that any treatment had helped Chad yet. He was informed that Chad was over 18 and they couldn't detain him against his will.

◆◆◆◆◆◆

```
          CANADIAN TIRE 467
        11907 KINGSWAY AVE EDMONTON AB T5G WY5
              780-413-0472

  REG 014 06/09/2000 15:22:44 TRANS #220
  OPERATOR 01 01

  67-6111-2    TAPE,CTHSEALTAH   $    1.09
  62-3501-2    HOSE KIT,SUMP 2   $    6.99
  93-5601-8    Icetea/Juice?si   $    1.29
  300          BOTTLE DEPOSIT    ¥    0.05

               SUBTOTAL          $    9.32
               G.S.T             $    0.65
               T O T A L         $    9.97
               CASH TEND.        $   10.00
               CHANGE            $    0.03
               BASE CT MONEY     $    0.20
          ORIGINAL RECEIPT AND CANADIAN TIRE
        MONEY REQUIRED FOR EXCHANGE OR REFUND
              THANK YOU FOR SHOPPING AT
              CANADIAN TIRE KINGSWAY
                STILL THE RIGHT PLACE!
                 GST#137946409
```

Received from Reçu de	Date June 9/00
Chad Stephen	
Three Hundred + Twenty-one $\frac{00}{100}$ Dollars	
198 Mercury Glen Marquis 2dr	
1MEBE84G4BZ642812 Black	

$ 321.00 $300 +$21 GST   Sold as is

Tax Reg. No.: 88120 3129 RT0001   No.
No d'enrg. taxe   Dawn Eber

77

THE TICKET

Chad:

The Darkest Hour

In the darkest hour

In the dead of the night

Your candle flickers

To reveal the light

The wind blows softly

In my darkest hour

The touch of your hand

So gently holds a greater power

To feel your touch

Can mean so much

In my darkest hour

I hear thunder

I feel the pain

I know the troubles

78

You keep in the rain

Sadly I whisper

And call out your name

In my darkest hour.

◆◆◆◆◆◆

Trent, I just wanted to tell you that I understand that you may never know why I did this. However, it really doesn't matter. Just know that, though it may not of seemed like it, I cannot remember a time in my life wherein I didn't feel some abnormal sense of stress or insecurity. The point is being you are a father, I want you to know that you have something I've always wanted. Please, do not take this responsibility lightly. I know I don't have to tell you this, but I hope you can always provide Victoria with not only her material needs but also, the support and proper guidance she will need to become an independent and confident young woman. This world is not by any stretch of the imagination getting to be an easier place to survive.

Regardless of what you may believe, I'm sure you are smart enough to know to try and shelter her from some of the things we have been exposed to. Those are the things that can make or break an individual's chance at a normal and productive life. What I mean is, just because you feel you may be able to function despite some of your habits, there are people who for reasons too numerous to explain, don't have the strength to juggle the pressures and what they conceive to be their ways of dealing with them.

I don't even know if you have a clue what I'm trying to say, but essentially...never hold Victoria too tight and never let her wander too far until you are sure she is strong enough in her own mind to choose the right path. Also, remember that path began four years ago and you have a major responsibility to guide her in the right direction until her coming of age (which can be defined by every moment you have any influence on her and the world around her).

THAT'S IT!

Hope to see you on the other side!

PS Forgive me if you cannot find it in yourself to understand and know that if there is a heaven (providing I make it there), I'll always be watching from above and your trials of life with and without your daughter will not be fought without a little help beyond.

Later dates,
Chad

◆◆◆◆◆◆

Yet, even today I can still hear the rustling of the wind blowing through the Saskatchewan wheat fields. What's more, I can't shake the sometimes haunting feeling of kinship and ancestry pulling me with a desperate longing and the notion that the immense pleasures and simplicity of a world I know live on in some far and distant place. For now, though I can only hope that what feels as real as the blood in my veins somewhere remains more than just the memory of a place and time, which to this day I carry with me wherever I go.

I must admit, I'm not really sure what's real anymore. At this point, all I really know is that approximately seven years ago I contracted quite a severe mononucleosis infection. Now everything since seems somewhat a blur.

Consequently, at present, my world consists of nothing but a seemingly constant and never ending platform of images and memories no longer connected to the emotions they once evoked. When thinking back on what seems right and wrong, or what feels good or bad, today these images seem nothing more than a constantly repeating slide show without beginning or end. One image after another image spins endlessly in some ever changing and undefined order, which I can only suspect, may somehow be connected to a similarly confused order of moods and an ever-changing grasp on reality. There is, however, the fluttering nuance of positive emotions I do recall, and contentment seem forever buried somewhere deep in the baggage that seems forever too heavy to carry on, to wherever it is I left behind my best and most comfortable outfit.

The trip is over. Please collect your baggage at the gate and have a nice day. Remember! Measure your wealth in friends and not in dollars. All the money in the world can not change the fact that we are no one unless someone loves or cares for us.

PS Don't forget to wear your sunscreen!

PS I, like many before me, with and after me, willfully believe that we are a trinity of mind, body and soul. Call me crazy. Call me anything you want; but never judge me for believing that for years I've felt that my mind and body is dying. Forgive me, but I just had to go before I lost the only thing still relatively intact...my soul!

R.I.P

Those who knew me knew
me as a prince among
men.
Those who knew me well
knew me as a king of fails;
but all and all I loved them
all just the same!

chad

P.S.
Candidiasis [illegible]
is CF

Please give to
my mom

◆◆◆◆◆◆

I drove about ten miles north of the city. Steering the car into a farmer's field, I parked on a small dirt road following the edge of the field. There were lots of glorious trees, branching out on both sides of the road and above my car. I had discovered a peaceful, secluded area where I could reunite with Mother Nature. I wrote a short note for Mom. Then I connected the hose to the Marquis.

I slid back into the car and flipped up the music on the radio. My cherished music would help me find peace.

HOUSE CALL

Mom: On June 13, 2000, my doorbell rang. Two policemen were standing there.

"Are you Lorri Starr?"

"Yes."

The other officer said "your son passed away."

"When?"

The officer responded "about 4:30 this afternoon."

"How?"

Constable Simms continued with "he died of acute carbon monoxide toxicity."

Tremulous and reeling I answered" I knew this would happen."

"What makes you say that?"

Sitting on the couch holding my head and staring vacantly at the floor "because suicide was all he talked about for the last eight years."

I felt so hollow. The officer inquired if I was all right and might he do anything for me.

I emptily replied, "No, I'm OK. I'll phone Chad's dad and brothers. Thanks for coming."

My landlord, Cal (a fellow with MS) was sleeping. Homecare workers came into settle him down in bed about 8 pm. I didn't even bother to wake him to tell him of my tragedy.

I gulped down a sleeping pill and went to bed to bawl my heart out. Unfortunately, crying in these circumstances won't cease in one night. I would mourn for my son for many years to come. I'm weeping now as I write this. Nothing will ever erase this pain.

◆◆◆◆◆◆

I had picked up Chad's clothing items at the funeral home. I examined each article to see if there was anything out of the ordinary. All I found was a bloodstain streaked down the front of his shirt. The blood capillaries of his nostrils had erupted after the carbon monoxide poisoning. I felt queasy looking at the stain. It was another reminder of how my son demised. His pants and wallet were missing.

Nobody seemed to know where Chad's pants and wallet had disappeared. I didn't need to have just anyone attain his personal belongings and doing who knows what with them.

Between the policemen who first identified Chad, the car pound, the medical examiner and the funeral home, no one could recall where the pants and wallet had disappeared. It was so frustrating, arguing with each of these people, day after day, over the disappearance of these items. Finally the police reassured me by entering Chad's name (in more than one spelling) on their computer files, as deceased. That way no one could try to filch his identity.

◆◆◆◆◆◆

Chad:

1) I wish that the guitar book Paul gave me this Christmas is given to Shane (telephone number in the book). I have never met or known anyone who inspired my musical interests as he did.

2) I wish that my rosary and left over gift certificates be given to my mother. She has been my only really constant companion as bad went to worse.

3) My briefcase itself, (the case), I wish to be left to my brother Trent. My mother gave it to me, hoping that one day I would be the one who would need it. Well, seeing as how I won't be using it, maybe his endeavours will provide the necessity. Also, give Trent my favourite watch. I hope he enjoys it as much as I did.

4) I wish that the audiocassette tapes and the case be given to my brother, Paul. I can only hope they are the right ones. If so, they probably have to be dubbed down from a higher speed multi-track recorder.

5) Finally, I wish that the pictures be given to my Dad, along with a copy of the song "4 A.M." by Our Lady Peace. Please, if possible also include a copy of the words to this song printed out with the recording.

Do what you wish with everything else. It means nothing to me. Candidadiasis is very real. If at all possible, my greatest wish is that the fungal infestation, predominately in the larger colon, be identified before (cremation) so that my suffering is not in vain.

P.S. Dr. G. is a pompous ass with a God complex. Do not listen to this man! In my opinion he should be removed from any position of authority over the care of mentally ill people.

Songs to remember:

1) 4 A.M. (Our Lady of Peace)

2) Time of Your Life (Greenday)

3) Too Much Love Will Kill You (Queen Made in Heaven)

4) I Remember You (Skid Row)

5) Fly to the Angels (Slaughter)

6) Angel (Sarah McLachlan)

◆◆◆◆◆◆

Mom: Chad wanted desperately to prove to everyone that Candidadiasis or some other intestinal disorder existed in his body. We did carry out his final wish, which was an autopsy. The autopsy of his chest and abdomen were performed. The medical examiner's report identified very little. Yes, there was mild inflammation of the bowel; a chronic abdominal pain was noted. Was this the origin of the beginning of the end? There was no sign of a systemic yeast infection. It seemed that in the end it was a pseudo-mental fixation that had convinced him to take his life.

REMEMBRANCE DAY

Mom: Ralph, Paul, Trent and I congregated at the Park Memorial Chapel the next morning. It was astounding to see how Trent directed control of the circumstances. Actually, I was relieved someone could see straight, so to speak. Trent was probably Chad's closest playmate while growing up. He appeared to understand what Chad would have been comfortable with.

Adam heard from Ken, one of Chad's friends. Thank goodness for that. Ken was on the phone immediately informing everyone who they could remember, who Chad knew, about Chad's funeral.

John was adamant about not going to Chad's funeral because of the pact they had made after Billy passed away. Adam and John fought over that. Adam still deemed John should attend.

Chad's brothers put together a collage of photos of Chad's life and his experiences, to hang at the front of the funeral home. Father Dodd baptized Chad and I now requested that he would perform the sacrament of helping Chad's soul enter into heaven.

I realize that there are people who do not understand the ways of the Lord, but I firmly believe that Chad received messages from heaven to build strength and endurance for himself in this world. I presented a short eulogy and then read a Psalm that we found in his belongings, torn from a bible.

Psalm 91

He who dwells in the shelter of the Most High

Will abide in the shadow of the Almighty.

I will say to the Lord "My refuge and my fortress,

My God, in whom I trust!"

For it is He who delivers you from the snare of the trapper,

And from the deadly pestilence.

He will cover with his pinions,

And under His wings you may seek refuge;

His faithfulness is a shield and bulwark.

You will not be afraid of the terror by night,

Or of the arrow that flies by day,

Of the pestilence that stalks in the darkness,

Or of the destruction that lays waste at noon.

A thousand may fall at your side,

And ten thousand at your right hand;

But it shall not approach you.

You will look only on with your eyes,

And see the recompense of the wicked.

For you have made the Lord, my refuge,

Even the Most High, your dwelling place.

No evil will befall you.

Nor will any plaque come near your tent.

For He will give His angels charge concerning you,

To guard you in all your ways.

They will bear you up in their hands,

That you do not strike your foot against a stone,

You will tread upon the lion and cobra,

The young lion and the serpent you will trample down.

Because he has loved Me, therefore I will deliver him;

I will set him securely on high, because he has known My name.

He will call upon Me, and I will answer him;

I will be with him in trouble;

I will rescue him, and honour him.

With a long life I will satisfy him,

And let him see my salvation.

◆◆◆◆◆◆

That's when I became aware of Chad's family and friends that were in attendance. I only hope that Chad's spirit was present to see how many people really did love him.

So many of Chad's friends had a hard time believing that the man in the coffin was Chad. The carbon monoxide in his body had distorted his handsome features. He appeared to be much heavier and bloated than in actual life.

His dad cried when he was born and he cried when he passed away. It was as if Chad's brief life of 27 years on earth had gone full circle.

We asked for donations to Chad's memory to be given to the Canadian Mental Health Association.

Most of our family and friends connected with us at Trent's house for a reception after the funeral. It was pleasant to be able to converse with a lot of our old friends, whom we hadn't set eyes on for years.

Trent prepared a delicious spread of tacos, chili, humus, raw vegetables and sauces. He was an experienced cook from working in various restaurants when he was younger.

A few photo albums were being flipped through, letting us reminisce. We showed a video of the immediate family during Chad's life. As the day carried on, the older folks left.

The younger people remained, moving to the back yard, where a bonfire was lit. There was an all night wake, until 7 or 8 a.m. Chad would have loved his last party.

◆◆◆◆◆

I kept the urn holding Chad's ashes on the top shelf of my bedroom closet. I couldn't bear to have my son away from me. Inside my heart, I felt he was still with me.

COMING BACK

About two months later I was watching television downstairs. The doorbell rang. The bell was set up with a distinctive ring just for the basement and a different ring for the upstairs suite. I hurried upstairs.

After opening the door and glancing around, there was no one to be seen. I returned to the basement and got comfortable on the couch again. Within 15 minutes, the doorbell rang for a second time. After dashing up the stairs again and opening the door, there was still no one around.

Somehow I had the feeling that Chad had returned in spirit to say "I'm OK Mom. Everything is all right now." Tears of pain and comfort spilled from my eyes.

◆◆◆◆◆◆

Ralph, Paul, Krista, Trent and I drove out to Brown-field on June 3, 2001. Ralph drove his car to the Mt. Vital Cemetery. I had just gone through lasik eye surgery and my vision was dreadfully blurry. I had finally made up my mind to lay Chad to rest and waiting until my eyes healed seemed to be too much of a delay. It was time to bury Chad's ashes.

The tombstone we selected was very appropriate. On it was inscribed a Christian verse, along side a picture of a field of grass. Now he would be able to be close to nature forever.

EPILOGUE

About a year later I was determined to chronicle Chad's life and embarked on interviewing people who knew Chad.

I met Shane at a lounge on the north side of the city. He had a beer, but I wasn't really a drinker, so I ordered a diet coke.

I used my camcorder to record our conversation, but I didn't aim the lens at either of us.

Shane related a dream so real it didn't seem like a dream to him. Shane was walking past a delicatessen and Chad was lying on the counter calling for Trent. This reminded Shane of Chad being laid out in the funeral home. It gave both of us the shivers as he told me.

Another time Chad appeared out of the blue to Shane. He was trying to tell Shane something but Shane didn't get it. Shane just kept bawling "Go away, you can't stay in limbo! You don't belong here!" After that last spiritual appearance, Chad never returned. Maybe it took that last statement from Shane to make Chad realize he had to cross over for good.

❖❖❖❖❖❖

After becoming baffled trying to locate Dr. Locke's office (I was 15 minutes late) I was approached by a very pleasant man. Dr. Locke and I strode down the hallway to his office.

He invited me to describe Chad. I quizzed "the good part or the bad part?"

I portrayed Chad as superbly intelligent and sociable. On the other hand he was sly and cunning. I conveyed the break into my safe for money and his thefts from Jean's garage.

In the latter years Chad appeared to have no concept that his AISH cheque was to cover a whole month's expenses. He would exhaust it all in one week and not realize it was necessary that he purchase groceries for three additional weeks. Then he would pilfer to obtain groceries and drugs.

Was it that Chad was bi-polar? As I scrutinized the behaviour of others with that illness, I realized that this was not the case. Two of Chad's relatives suffered with schizophrenia. I showed Dr. Locke Chad's poem "Spirit Guide" and inquired if he thought it pointed to schizophrenia. Dr. Locke didn't consider that so, unless it was in the "grey" area (where a definite diagnosis could not be made because symptoms weren't yet apparent).

Dr. Locke asked what I thought was amiss with Chad. I sensed he just didn't want to grow up, even after I evicted him from my home at 27 years old.

The hospital also strived to encourage Chad to grow up and take responsibility for himself. If Chad was informed that he could dwell in the hospital for the rest of his life, he would have been content with that. I tried everything I could to get Chad to mature. He had been a patient in the hospital

72 times, even though he wasn't fortunate enough to be an inpatient every time.

The doctor suggested that Chad had such a strong bond with me that the bond seemed more powerful than Chad himself. It was as if Chad was still attached to my umbilical cord and wouldn't let go. I accepted this theory as factual.

Dr. Locke and I agreed on the only diagnosis we could arrive at...deep depression. Chad repeatedly accused the doctors of naming his condition "psychosomatic".

Just before parting from the doctor's office, Dr. Locke suggested Chad's suicide might possibly have been his final argument to his "intestinal disorder" as if "do the biopsy now...see the proof". The doctor expressed gratitude to me for providing him with insights to Chad's behaviour. He also affirmed that Chad's passing touched everyone that was acquainted with him at the hospital.

*WHERE TO LOOK
FOR HELP

Contact numbers are on the red-bordered front emergency pages of your white pages Edmonton telephone book.